Published by Creative Education and
Creative Paperbacks
P.O. Box 227, Mankato, Minnesota 56002
Creative Education and Creative Paperbacks
are imprints of The Creative Company
www.thecreativecompany.us

Design by The Design Lab
Production by Chelsey Luther
Art direction by Rita Marshall
Printed in the United States of America

Photographs by Alamy (Greatstock, imageBROKER,
Ivan Kuzmin), Dreamstime (Isselee), FreeVectorMaps.
com, Getty Images (Education Images), iStockphoto
(aimee1065, bondgrunge), National Geographic
Creative (Frans Lanting), Shutterstock (jo Crebbin,
Dennis W Donohue, ernstc, Elsa Hoffmann, Andrzej
Kubik, wectors)

Library of Congress Cataloging-in-Publication Data
Names: Riggs, Kate.
Title: Ostriches / Kate Riggs.
Series: Amazing Animals.
Includes bibliographical references and index.
Summary: A basic exploration of the appearance,
behavior, and habitat of ostriches, the tall, fast-
running African birds. Also included is a story from
folklore explaining why ostriches keep their wings
close to the body.
Identifiers: ISBN 978-1-60818-880-2 (hardcover)
/ ISBN 978-1-62832-496-9 (pbk) / ISBN 978-1-
56660-932-6 (eBook)

This title has been submitted for CIP processing under
LCCN 2017937492.

CCSS: RI.1.1, 2, 4, 5, 6, 7; RI.2.2, 5, 6, 7, 10;
RI.3.1, 5, 7, 8; RF.1.1, 3, 4; RF.2.3, 4

First Edition HC 9 8 7 6 5 4 3 2 1
First Edition PBK 9 8 7 6 5 4 3 2 1

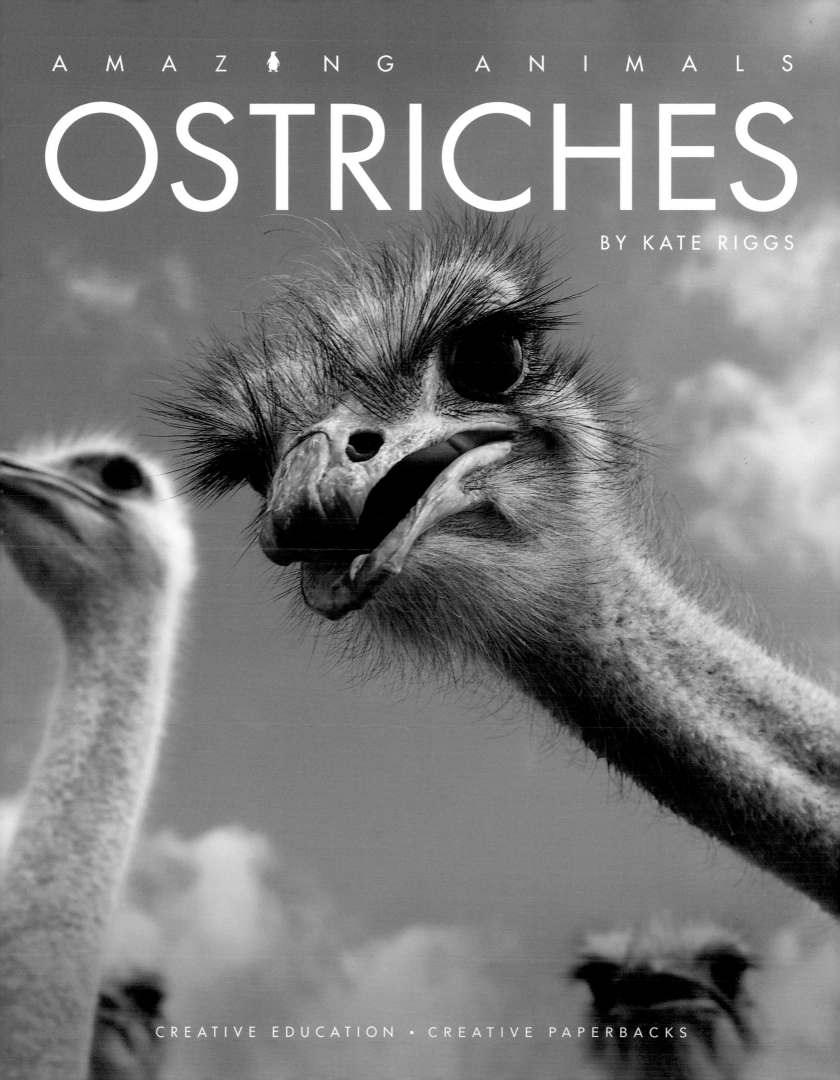

AMAZING ANIMALS

OSTRICHES

BY KATE RIGGS

CREATIVE EDUCATION • CREATIVE PAPERBACKS

Long-legged ostriches are the largest birds in the world

Ostriches are large birds from Africa. There are two ostrich **species**. These birds cannot fly. But they can run fast. Their top speed is 45 miles (72.4 km) per hour.

species a group of similar (or closely related) animals

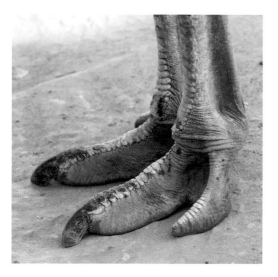

Many ostriches have pink necks and legs. The Somali ostrich is gray-blue instead. Ostrich legs are powerful. One kick could break a lion's back!

Ostriches have two forward-facing toes on each foot (above)

The red-necked ostrich stands nine feet (2.7 m) tall. It weighs more than 300 pounds (136 kg). Other ostriches are seven to eight feet (2.1–2.4 m) tall. Their size keeps other animals away. Male and female ostriches have different-colored feathers.

Adult males have darker feathers that catch females' attention

Ostriches live on hot African grasslands. Their large eyes look around for dangers. They also look for food.

Ostriches are almost always on the move in their habitats

Long, fine feathers keep dust away from ostriches' large eyes

Grasses and other plants feed ostriches. They also eat **insects**. Adult ostriches eat about seven pounds (3.2 kg) of food each day. They do not need to drink much water.

insects small animals with three body parts and six legs

Hatchlings are about the size of full-grown chickens

A female ostrich lays about 12 eggs. The **hatchlings** must be strong to break through the eggshells. They have fluffy feathers called down at first. Young ostriches watch their parents. They learn what foods to eat.

hatchlings baby ostriches that have just come out of their eggs

Young ostriches stay in their first family group for two or three years

Ostriches spend part of the year in herds. These family groups have up to 50 members. Herds take care of the youngest birds. These are easier **prey** for baboons, lions, jackals, and leopards. Ostriches can live about 30 years in the wild.

prey animals that are killed and eaten by other animals

*Ostriches' wings help
them turn sharply
while running*

Ostrich eyes can see up to 2.5 miles (4 km) away. They know when they have time to hide. Or they start running. Running in a group helps ostriches confuse **predators**.

predators animals that kill and eat other animals

People can see ostriches in zoos or on farms. Sometimes, people who visit Africa may see ostriches in the wild. It is exciting to see these long-legged birds run!

Short, soft feathers cover an ostrich's neck and head

An Ostrich Story

Why do ostriches hold their wings so close to their bodies?

People in Africa told a story about this. Ostrich loved learning new things. But he kept everything secret. When Ostrich found out about fire, he tucked it under his wing. Mantis saw that Ostrich kept fire there. He tricked Ostrich into dropping the fire. Then Mantis shared it with people. Ostrich has held his wings close to his body ever since.

Read More

Schuetz, Kari. *Ostriches*. Minneapolis: Bellwether Media, 2013.

Schuh, Mari. *The World's Biggest Birds*. Minneapolis: Jump!, 2016.

Websites

Enchanted Learning: Ostrich
http://www.enchantedlearning.com/subjects/birds/printouts/Ostrichcoloring.shtml
This site has ostrich facts and a picture to color.

National Geographic Kids: Ostrich
http://kids.nationalgeographic.com/animals/ostrich/#ostrich-grass.jpg
Learn more about ostriches!

Note: Every effort has been made to ensure that the websites listed above are suitable for children, that they have educational value, and that they contain no inappropriate material. However, because of the nature of the Internet, it is impossible to guarantee that these sites will remain active indefinitely or that their contents will not be altered.

Index